THE GREAT OUTDOORS
FISHING

By E. T. Weingarten

Gareth Stevens
Publishing

Please visit our website, www.garethstevens.com. For a free color catalog of all our high-quality books, call toll free 1-800-542-2595 or fax 1-877-542-2596.

Library of Congress Cataloging-in-Publication Data

Weingarten, E. T.
Fishing / E.T. Weingarten.
    p. cm. — (The great outdoors)
Includes index.
ISBN 978-1-4339-7096-2 (pbk.)
ISBN 978-1-4339-7097-9 (6-pack)
ISBN 978-1-4339-7095-5 (library binding)
1. Fishing—Juvenile literature. I. Title.
SH445.W396 2013
639.2—dc23

                                        2011047930

First Edition

Published in 2013 by
Gareth Stevens Publishing
111 East 14th Street, Suite 349
New York, NY 10003

Copyright © 2013 Gareth Stevens Publishing

Designer: Michael J. Flynn
Editor: Therese Shea

Photo credits: Cover, p. 1, iStockphoto.com/Sean Boogs; p. 5 iStockphoto.com/dannay79; p. 6 (main) Gorilla/Shutterstock.com; p. 6 (inset) RWBrooks/Shutterstock.com; p. 9 pinponpix/ Shutterstock.com; p. 10 (main) Julian Rovagnati/Shutterstock.com, p. 10 (inset) GWImages; p. 13 (main) Csaba Peterdi/Shutterstock.com; p. 13 (inset) bogdan ionescu/Shutterstock.com; p. 14 (popper) Petr Malyshev/Shutterstock.com; p. 14 (spinner) Zheltyshev/Shutterstock.com; p. 14 (plug) Fedor Kondratenko/Shutterstock.com; p. 14 (spoon) David Brimm/Shutterstock.com; p. 14 (jig) Krasowit/Shutterstock.com; p. 15 Andy Lidstone/Shutterstock.com; p. 17 Dani Vincek/ Shutterstock.com; p. 18 Jessica Bethke/Shutterstock.com; p. 20 bikeriderlonden/Shutterstock.com; p. 21 iofoto/Shutterstock.com.

Printed in the United States of America

CPSIA compliance information: Batch #CS12GS: For further information contact Gareth Stevens, New York, New York at 1-800-542-2595.

CONTENTS

Words in the glossary appear in **bold** type the first time they are used in the text.

WHAT A CATCH!

You're sitting in a boat, watching warm sunshine sparkle on the water. A fishing rod is in your hands and a line is in the water. Suddenly, you feel a little tug, then a stronger one. The fishing rod bends toward the water while you struggle to **reel** in the line. Finally, you see what's on your hook—a huge fish!

The sport of fishing is about both relaxation and excitement. It's for everyone, young and old. It's a perfect way to spend time in the great outdoors!

Fishing is a sport for some and a business for others. It's also a way to catch your own food.

5

angling

It's important to have the right fishing rod. Most anglers don't need a heavy rod – unless they're trying to catch a real whopper!

spearfishing

ANGLERS

Different fishing gear, or tackle, is needed for different kinds of fishing. Some people use **spears** or nets to catch fish, but most use rods. People who use rods, reels, and lines to catch fish are called anglers. It doesn't have to cost a lot of money to be an angler.

A fishing rod can be as simple as a wooden stick. However, people usually buy lightweight rods made of stronger **materials**, such as aluminum or **fiberglass**. The rod should bend, but not snap, when weighed down by a big fish.

INTO THE WILD

Scientists think that people started making tools to fish more than 35,000 years ago!

LINES AND REELS

Many fishing lines are clear so fish can't see them. However, colored lines better match some waters. A single strand of fishing line is called monofilament. Nylon is a popular material used to make monofilament.

Fishing line is stored in a reel. Many reels have a metal half loop called a bail that opens to let the line out. The line is neatly wound back into the reel by turning the reel's handle.

INTO THE WILD

Many fishing lines are measured by the weight they can bear. Lines may hold up to 200 pounds (91 kg). Some fishing lines are made of twisted strands for extra strength.

There are different kinds of reels for different kinds of fishing. Some help anglers throw the line, or cast, great distances.

9

The barb on a hook is the point facing away from the head of the hook. A barb keeps the hook in place after a fish is caught.

leader

HOOKS AND LEADERS

Fishhooks are a shape that won't easily slip out of a fish's mouth. A hook may be tied to the end of a line, or it may be attached to a leader. A leader is a short piece of fishing line that's tied to the end of the main line.

Why do some anglers use leaders? A leader of a different color than the main line may blend in better with the water. Also, leaders made of stronger line are used to catch saltwater fish that cut monofilament with their teeth, such as bluefish and mackerel.

INTO THE WILD

Fishhooks differ with kinds of fishing. Some hooks are meant to keep bait alive. Others look like flies and other tasty meals for fish.

SINKERS AND FLOATS

Sinkers are objects attached to fishing line that sink bait. Sinkers also add weight so a line can be cast farther away. Sinkers may weigh as much as 3 pounds (1.4 kg).

An angler needs a float in addition to a sinker to catch fish that don't swim at the bottom. Floats are made out of materials such as cork and plastic. Floats also help anglers keep their hooks from getting stuck in rocks and grass at the bottom of the water.

INTO THE WILD

A creel is a container that keeps fish fresh after they're caught.

Sometimes floats are called bobbers. When a fish grabs the line, the float "bobs" up and down in the water.

sinkers

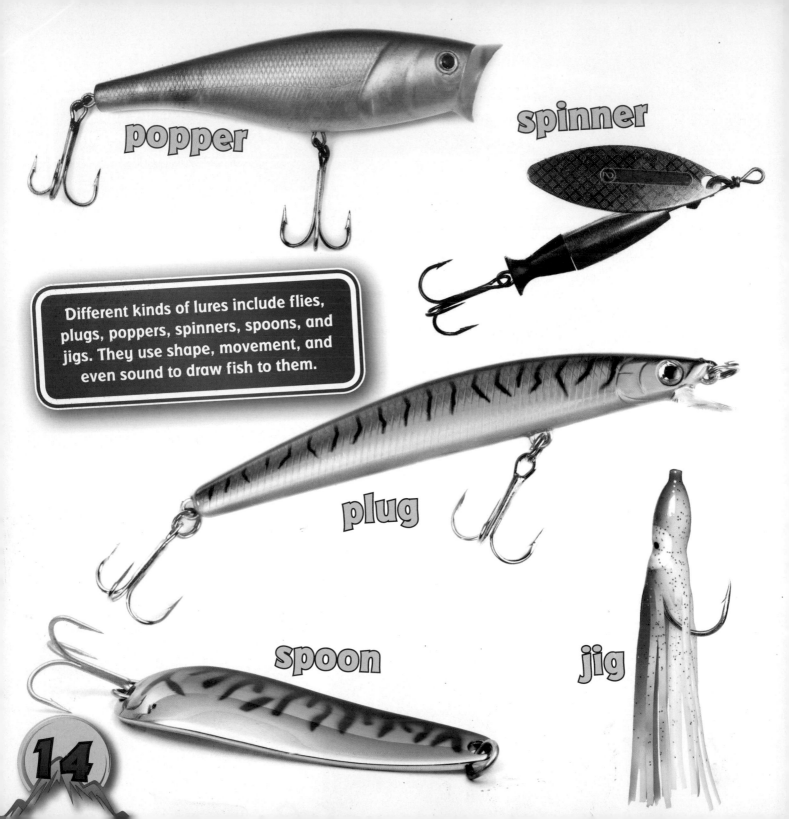

popper

spinner

Different kinds of lures include flies, plugs, poppers, spinners, spoons, and jigs. They use shape, movement, and even sound to draw fish to them.

plug

spoon

jig

14

ON THE HOOK

So what do you put on a fishhook? Whatever a fish likes to eat! Many freshwater and saltwater fish eat worms and smaller fish, such as minnows and **anchovies**. Sometimes anglers use live bait, but bits of dead fish may work well, too.

Some anglers use bait that isn't real. Lures are made of feathers, yarn, hair, or other materials. They look like bait, and some even move in the water like a tasty, fishy treat! A lure can be used many times, unlike fresh bait.

fly

INTO THE WILD

Some freshwater fish, such as carp, eat cheese!

KINDS OF FISHING

Some kinds of fishing require boats. Deep-sea anglers need a large boat with a motor that can handle big waves on the ocean. They also need heavy-duty rods and strong lines for large catches. Saltwater fishing in shallow water is called flats fishing.

Pier fishing requires no boat. Anglers cast off piers to catch fish that like to be near shore. In fly-fishing, people use long rods and special lures to catch trout and other fish in streams and rivers.

INTO THE WILD

Some people like to fish in winter through a hole in the ice over the water. Ice fishing can be dangerous if the ice is too thin.

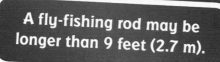

A fly-fishing rod may be longer than 9 feet (2.7 m).

17

OVERFISHING

Some fish are in danger of dying out because they've been overfished. Anglers may only be allowed to catch and keep a small number of them at certain times of the year. At any other time, the fish have to be thrown back. As another way to **protect** fish populations, many areas require people to have a **license** to fish.

Protecting fish is an important part of keeping **ecosystems** healthy. The disappearance of just one kind of fish can have terrible effects on the living things that depend on them.

NO FISHING BEYOND THIS POINT

OVERFISHING

Why It's a Problem

- fish help other fish to stay alive
- fish keep ecosystems healthy
- people depend on fish for food and business

Ways to Stop It

- require fishing licenses
- limit the number of fish caught
- limit catching fish to certain times of year

19

GO FISH!

Anglers try to learn as much as they can about the fish they want to catch. Do they swim near the bottom or the surface? Do they like cold or warm water? At what time of day do they feed? However, the great thing about fishing is that anyone can do it, even without knowing the answers to these questions.

Charter boats often let people fish under a special license, rent fishing tackle, and even prepare fish for eating. If this sounds fun, then what are you waiting for? Go fish!

Most fish are more active in the early morning and in the evening, when there's low light.

21

GLOSSARY

anchovy: a small silver fish that travels in large schools

charter boat: a boat that can be hired for a special use, such as fishing or sightseeing

ecosystem: a community of living things and their surroundings

fiberglass: glass fibers pressed into a hard material. Often used in construction.

license: official permission from the government to do something

material: matter used to make things

pier: a structure that extends out over a body of water

protect: to guard

reel: to wind up a fishing line. Also, a wheel-shaped tool around which fishing line is wound.

spear: a weapon for throwing or attacking that has a long handle and a sharp point

FOR MORE INFORMATION

BOOKS

Klein, Adam G. *Fishing*. Edina, MN: ABDO Publishing, 2008.

Lundgren, Julie K. *Fishing*. Vero Beach, FL: Rourke Publishing, 2010.

WEBSITES

Fish

animals.nationalgeographic.com/animals/fish/
Find out about many kinds of fish, both big and small.

Fishing Fun

www.americaoutdoors.com/fishing/fishing_fun/
Read a fishing comic strip.

Fish Kids

www.epa.gov/waterscience/fish/kids/
Learn more about fish and fishing while playing games.

Publisher's note to educators and parents: Our editors have carefully reviewed these websites to ensure that they are suitable for students. Many websites change frequently, however, and we cannot guarantee that a site's future contents will continue to meet our high standards of quality and educational value. Be advised that students should be closely supervised whenever they access the Internet.

INDEX